DOMINUS IESUS

DECLARATION
on the unicity and salvific universality
of Jesus Christ and the Church

"This document expresses once again the same
ecumenical passion that is the basis of my encyclical *Ut Unum Sint*. I hope this Declaration,
which is close to my heart, can, after so many
erroneous interpretations, finally fulfill its function both of clarification and openness"

Pope *St. John Paul II*

DOMINUS IESUS, Declaration on the Unicity and Salvific Universality of Jesus Christ and the Church
English translation copyright © 2000 Libreria Editrice Vaticana. All rights reserved. Used with permission.

ISBN: 978-1-365-94721-6

This is an official document of the Catholic Church first published August 6th, 2000 by the *Congregation for the Doctrine of the Faith*, the Vatican office established "to promote and safeguard the doctrine on the faith and morals throughout the Catholic world". It is intended to be distributed without restrictions. The English text presented here is of Public Domain and was taken from http://www.vatican.va/roman_curia/congregations/cfaith/documents/rc_con_cfaith_-doc_20000806_dominus-iesus_en.html, Web May 7th 2017.

Comments, suggestions and/or corrections to press_in@yahoo.com

Table of Contents

INTRODUCTION

1. The *Lord Jesus,* before ascending into heaven, commanded his disciples to proclaim the Gospel to the whole world and to baptize all nations: "Go into the whole world and proclaim the Gospel to every creature. He who believes and is baptized will be saved; he who does not believe will be condemned" (*Mk* 16:15-16); "All power in heaven and on earth has been given to me. Go therefore and teach all nations, baptizing them in the name of the Father, and of the Son, and of the Holy Spirit, teaching them to observe all that I have commanded you. And behold, I am with you always, until the end of the world" (*Mt* 28:18-20; cf. *Lk* 24:46-48; *Jn* 17:18,20,21; *Acts* 1:8).

The Church's universal mission is born from the command of Jesus Christ and is fulfilled in the course of the centuries in the proclamation of the mystery of God, Father, Son, and Holy Spirit, and the mystery of the incarnation of the Son, as saving event for all humanity. The fundamental contents of the profession of the Christian faith are expressed thus:

"I believe in one God, the Father, Almighty, maker of heaven and earth, of all that is, seen and unseen. I believe in one Lord, Jesus Christ, the only Son of God, eternally begotten of the Father, God from God, Light from Light, true God from true God, begotten, not made, of one being with the Father. Through him all things were made. For us men and for our salvation, he came down from heaven: by the power of the Holy Spirit he became incarnate of the Virgin Mary, and became man. For our sake he was crucified under Pontius Pilate; he suffered death and was buried. On the third day he rose again in accordance with the Scriptures; he ascended into heaven and is seated at the right hand of the Father. He will come again in glory to judge the living and the dead, and his kingdom will have no end. I believe in the Holy Spirit, the Lord, the giver of life, who proceeds from the Father. With the Father and the Son he is worshipped and glorified. He has spoken through the prophets. I believe in one holy catholic and apostolic Church. I acknowledge one baptism for the forgiveness of sins. I look for the resurrection of the dead, and the life of the world to come".[1]

2.   In the course of the centuries, the Church has proclaimed and witnessed with fidelity to the Gospel of Jesus. At the close of the second millennium, however, this mission is still far from complete.[2] For that reason, Saint Paul's

words are now more relevant than ever: "Preaching the Gospel is not a reason for me to boast; it is a necessity laid on me: woe to me if I do not preach the Gospel!" (*1 Cor* 9:16). This explains the Magisterium's particular attention to giving reasons for and supporting the evangelizing mission of the Church, above all in connection with the religious traditions of the world.[3]

In considering the values which these religions witness to and offer humanity, with an open and positive approach, the Second Vatican Council's Declaration on the relation of the Church to non-Christian religions states: "The Catholic Church rejects nothing of what is true and holy in these religions. She has a high regard for the manner of life and conduct, the precepts and teachings, which, although differing in many ways from her own teaching, nonetheless often reflect a ray of that truth which enlightens all men".[4] Continuing in this line of thought, the Church's proclamation of Jesus Christ, "the way, the truth, and the life" (*Jn* 14:6), today also makes use of the practice of inter-religious dialogue. Such dialogue certainly does not replace, but rather accompanies the *missio ad gentes*, directed toward that "mystery of unity", from which "it follows that all men and women who are saved share, though differently, in the same mystery of salvation in Jesus Christ through his Spirit".[5] Inter-religious dialogue, which is part of the Church's evangelizing mission,[6] requires an attitude of understanding and a relationship of mutual knowledge and reciprocal enrichment, in obedience to the truth and with respect for freedom.[7]

3. In the practice of dialogue between the Christian faith and other religious traditions, as well as in seeking to understand its theoretical basis more deeply, new questions arise that need to be addressed through pursuing new paths of research, advancing proposals, and suggesting ways of acting that call for attentive discernment. In this task, the present Declaration seeks to recall to Bishops, theologians, and all the Catholic faithful, certain indispensable elements of Christian doctrine, which may help theological reflection in developing solutions consistent with the contents of the faith and responsive to the pressing needs of contemporary culture.

The expository language of the Declaration corresponds to its purpose, which is not to treat in a systematic manner the question of the unicity and salvific universality of the mystery of Jesus Christ and the Church, nor to propose solutions to questions that are matters of free theological debate, but rather to set forth again the doctrine of the Catholic faith in these areas, pointing out some fundamental questions that remain open to further development, and refuting specific positions that are erroneous or ambiguous. For this reason, the Declaration takes up what has been taught in previous Magisterial documents, in order to reiterate certain truths that are part of the Church's faith.

4.   The Church's constant missionary proclamation is endangered today by relativistic theories which seek to justify religious pluralism, not only *de facto* but also *de iure (or in principle)*. As a consequence, it is held that certain truths have been superseded; for example, the definitive and complete character of the revelation of Jesus Christ, the nature of Christian faith as compared with that of belief in other religions, the inspired nature of the books of Sacred Scripture, the personal unity between the Eternal Word and Jesus of Nazareth, the unity of the economy of the Incarnate Word and the Holy Spirit, the unicity and salvific universality of the mystery of Jesus Christ, the universal salvific mediation of the Church, the inseparability — while recognizing the distinction — of the kingdom of God, the kingdom of Christ, and the Church, and the subsistence of the one Church of Christ in the Catholic Church.

The roots of these problems are to be found in certain presuppositions of both a philosophical and theological nature, which hinder the understanding and acceptance of the revealed truth. Some of these can be mentioned: the conviction of the elusiveness and inexpressibility of divine truth, even by Christian revelation; relativistic attitudes toward truth itself, according to which what is true for some would not be true for others; the radical opposition posited between the logical mentality of the West and the symbolic mentality of the East; the subjectivism which, by regarding reason as the only source of knowledge, becomes incapable of raising its "gaze to the heights, not daring to rise to the truth of being";[8] the difficulty in understanding and accepting the presence of definitive and eschatological events in history; the metaphysical emptying of the historical incarnation of the Eternal Logos, reduced to a mere appearing of God in history; the eclecticism of those who, in theological research, uncritically absorb ideas from a variety of philosophical and theological contexts without regard for consistency, systematic connection, or compatibility with Christian truth; finally, the tendency to read and to interpret Sacred Scripture outside the Tradition and Magisterium of the Church.

On the basis of such presuppositions, which may evince different nuances, certain theological proposals are developed — at times presented as assertions, and at times as hypotheses — in which Christian revelation and the mystery of Jesus Christ and the Church lose their character of absolute truth and salvific universality, or at least shadows of doubt and uncertainty are cast upon them.

I. THE FULLNESS AND DEFINITIVENESS OF THE REVELATION OF JESUS CHRIST

5.   As a remedy for this relativistic mentality, which is becoming ever more common, it is necessary above all to reassert the definitive and complete character of the revelation of Jesus Christ. In fact, it must be *firmly believed* that, in the mystery of Jesus Christ, the Incarnate Son of God, who is "the way, the truth, and the life" (*Jn* 14:6), the full revelation of divine truth is given: "No one knows the Son except the Father, and no one knows the Father except the Son and anyone to whom the Son wishes to reveal him" (*Mt* 11:27); "No one has ever seen God; God the only Son, who is in the bosom of the Father, has revealed him" (*Jn* 1:18); "For in Christ the whole fullness of divinity dwells in bodily form" (*Col* 2:9-10).

Faithful to God's word, the Second Vatican Council teaches: "By this revelation then, the deepest truth about God and the salvation of man shines forth in Christ, who is at the same time the mediator and the fullness of all revelation".[9] Furthermore, "Jesus Christ, therefore, the Word made flesh, sent 'as a man to men', 'speaks the words of God' (*Jn* 3:34), and completes the work of salvation which his Father gave him to do (cf. *Jn* 5:36; 17:4). To see Jesus is to see his Father (cf. *Jn* 14:9). For this reason, Jesus perfected revelation by fulfilling it through his whole work of making himself present and manifesting himself: through his words and deeds, his signs and wonders, but especially through his death and glorious resurrection from the dead and finally with the sending of the Spirit of truth, he completed and perfected revelation and confirmed it with divine testimony... The Christian dispensation, therefore, as the new and definitive covenant, will never pass away, and we now await no further new public revelation before the glorious manifestation of our Lord Jesus Christ (cf. *1 Tim* 6:14 and *Tit* 2:13)".[10]

Thus, the Encyclical *Redemptoris missio* calls the Church once again to the task of announcing the Gospel as the fullness of truth: "In this definitive Word of his revelation, God has made himself known in the fullest possible way. He has revealed to mankind who he is. This definitive self-revelation of God is the fundamental reason why the Church is missionary by her very nature. She cannot do other than proclaim the Gospel, that is, the fullness of the truth which God has enabled us to know about himself".[11] Only the revelation of Jesus Christ, therefore, "introduces into our history a universal and ultimate truth which stirs the human mind to ceaseless effort".[12]

6.   Therefore, the theory of the limited, incomplete, or imperfect character of the revelation of Jesus Christ, which would be complementary to that found in other religions, is contrary to the Church's faith. Such a position would claim to be based on the notion that the truth about God cannot

be grasped and manifested in its globality and completeness by any historical religion, neither by Christianity nor by Jesus Christ.

Such a position is in radical contradiction with the foregoing statements of Catholic faith according to which the full and complete revelation of the salvific mystery of God is given in Jesus Christ. Therefore, the words, deeds, and entire historical event of Jesus, though limited as human realities, have nevertheless the divine Person of the Incarnate Word, "true God and true man"[13] as their subject. For this reason, they possess in themselves the definitiveness and completeness of the revelation of God's salvific ways, even if the depth of the divine mystery in itself remains transcendent and inexhaustible. The truth about God is not abolished or reduced because it is spoken in human language; rather, it is unique, full, and complete, because he who speaks and acts is the Incarnate Son of God. Thus, faith requires us to profess that the Word made flesh, in his entire mystery, who moves from incarnation to glorification, is the source, participated but real, as well as the fulfillment of every salvific revelation of God to humanity,[14] and that the Holy Spirit, who is Christ's Spirit, will teach this "entire truth" (*Jn* 16:13) to the Apostles and, through them, to the whole Church.

7. The proper response to God's revelation is *"the obedience of faith* (*Rom* 16:26; cf. *Rom* 1:5; *2 Cor* 10:5-6) by which

man freely entrusts his entire self to God, offering 'the full submission of intellect and will to God who reveals' and freely assenting to the revelation given by him".[15] Faith is a gift of grace: "in order to have faith, the grace of God must come first and give assistance; there must also be the interior helps of the Holy Spirit, who moves the heart and converts it to God, who opens the eyes of the mind and gives 'to everyone joy and ease in assenting to and believing in the truth'".[16]

The obedience of faith implies acceptance of the truth of Christ's revelation, guaranteed by God, who is Truth itself:[17] "Faith is first of all a personal adherence of man to God. At the same time, and inseparably, it is a *free assent to the whole truth that God has revealed*".[18] Faith, therefore, as "*a gift of God*" and as "*a supernatural virtue infused by him*",[19] involves a dual adherence: to God who reveals and to the truth which he reveals, out of the trust which one has in him who speaks. Thus, "we must believe in no one but God: the Father, the Son and the Holy Spirit".[20]

For this reason, the distinction between *theological faith* and *belief* in the other religions, must be *firmly held*. If faith is the acceptance in grace of revealed truth, which "makes it possible to penetrate the mystery in a way that allows us to understand it coherently",[21] then belief, in the other religions, is that sum of experience and thought that constitutes the human treasury of wisdom and religious aspiration, which man in his search for truth has conceived and acted upon in his relationship to God and the Absolute.[22]

This distinction is not always borne in mind in current theological reflection. Thus, theological faith (the acceptance of the truth revealed by the One and Triune God) is often identified with belief in other religions, which is religious experience still in search of the absolute truth and still lacking assent to God who reveals himself. This is one of the reasons why the differences between Christianity and the other religions tend to be reduced at times to the point of disappearance.

8. The hypothesis of the inspired value of the sacred writings of other religions is also put forward. Certainly, it must be recognized that there are some elements in these texts which may be *de facto* instruments by which countless people throughout the centuries have been and still are able today to nourish and maintain their life-relationship with God. Thus, as noted above, the Second Vatican Council, in considering the customs, precepts, and teachings of the other religions, teaches that "although differing in many ways from her own teaching, these nevertheless often reflect a ray of that truth which enlightens all men".[23]

The Church's tradition, however, reserves the designation of *inspired texts* to the canonical books of the Old and New Testaments, since these are inspired by the Holy Spirit.[24] Taking up this tradition, the Dogmatic Constitution on

Divine Revelation of the Second Vatican Council states: "For Holy Mother Church, relying on the faith of the apostolic age, accepts as sacred and canonical the books of the Old and New Testaments, whole and entire, with all their parts, on the grounds that, written under the inspiration of the Holy Spirit (cf. *Jn* 20:31; *2 Tim* 3:16; *2 Pet* 1:19-21; 3:15-16), they have God as their author, and have been handed on as such to the Church herself".[25] These books "firmly, faithfully, and without error, teach that truth which God, for the sake of our salvation, wished to see confided to the Sacred Scriptures".[26]

Nevertheless, God, who desires to call all peoples to himself in Christ and to communicate to them the fullness of his revelation and love, "does not fail to make himself present in many ways, not only to individuals, but also to entire peoples through their spiritual riches, of which their religions are the main and essential expression even when they contain 'gaps, insufficiencies and errors'".[27] Therefore, the sacred books of other religions, which in actual fact direct and nourish the existence of their followers, receive from the mystery of Christ the elements of goodness and grace which they contain.

II. THE INCARNATE LOGOS AND THE HOLY SPIRIT IN THE WORK OF SALVATION

9.   In contemporary theological reflection there often emerges an approach to Jesus of Nazareth that considers him a particular, finite, historical figure, who reveals the divine not in an exclusive way, but in a way complementary with other revelatory and salvific figures. The Infinite, the Absolute, the Ultimate Mystery of God would thus manifest itself to humanity in many ways and in many historical figures: Jesus of Nazareth would be one of these. More concretely, for some, Jesus would be one of the many faces which the Logos has assumed in the course of time to communicate with humanity in a salvific way.

Furthermore, to justify the universality of Christian salvation as well as the fact of religious pluralism, it has been proposed that there is an economy of the eternal Word that is valid also outside the Church and is unrelated to her, in addition to an economy of the incarnate Word. The first would have a greater universal value than the second, which is limited to Christians, though God's presence would be more full in the second.

10.   These theses are in profound conflict with the Christian faith. The doctrine of faith must be *firmly believed* which proclaims that Jesus of Nazareth, son of Mary, and he alone, is the Son and the Word of the Father. The Word,

which "was in the beginning with God" (*Jn* 1:2) is the same as he who "became flesh" (*Jn* 1:14). In Jesus, "the Christ, the Son of the living God" (*Mt* 16:16), "the whole fullness of divinity dwells in bodily form" (*Col* 2:9). He is the "only begotten Son of the Father, who is in the bosom of the Father" (*Jn* 1:18), his "beloved Son, in whom we have redemption... In him the fullness of God was pleased to dwell, and through him, God was pleased to reconcile all things to himself, on earth and in the heavens, making peace by the blood of his Cross" (*Col* 1:13-14; 19-20).

Faithful to Sacred Scripture and refuting erroneous and reductive interpretations, the First Council of Nicaea solemnly defined its faith in: "Jesus Christ, the Son of God, the only begotten generated from the Father, that is, from the being of the Father, God from God, Light from Light, true God from true God, begotten, not made, one in being with the Father, through whom all things were made, those in heaven and those on earth. For us men and for our salvation, he came down and became incarnate, was made man, suffered, and rose again on the third day. He ascended to the heavens and shall come again to judge the living and the dead".[28] Following the teachings of the Fathers of the Church, the Council of Chalcedon also professed: "the one and the same Son, our Lord Jesus Christ, the same perfect in divinity and perfect in humanity, the same truly God and truly man..., one in being with the Father according to the divinity and one in being with us according to the humanity..., begotten of the Father before the ages according to the divinity and, in these last days, for us and our salvation, of Mary, the Virgin Mother of God, according to the humanity".[29]

For this reason, the Second Vatican Council states that Christ "the new Adam...'image of the invisible God' (Col 1:15) is himself the perfect man who has restored that likeness to God in the children of Adam which had been disfigured since the first sin... As an innocent lamb he merited life for us by his blood which he freely shed. In him God reconciled us to himself and to one another, freeing us from the bondage of the devil and of sin, so that each one of us could say with the apostle: the Son of God 'loved me and gave himself up for me' (Gal 2:20)".[30]

In this regard, John Paul II has explicitly declared: "To introduce any sort of separation between the Word and Jesus Christ is contrary to the Christian faith... Jesus is the Incarnate Word — a single and indivisible person... Christ is none other than Jesus of Nazareth; he is the Word of God made man for the salvation of all... In the process of discovering and appreciating the manifold gifts — especially the spiritual treasures — that God has bestowed on every people, we cannot separate those gifts from Jesus Christ, who is at the centre of God's plan of salvation".[31]

It is likewise contrary to the Catholic faith to introduce a separation between the salvific action of the Word as such and that of the Word made man. With the incarnation, all the salvific actions of the Word of God are always done in unity with the human nature that he has assumed for the salvation of all people. The one subject which operates in the two natures, human and divine, is the single person of the Word.[32]

Therefore, the theory which would attribute, after the incarnation as well, a salvific activity to the Logos as such in his divinity, exercised "in addition to" or "beyond" the humanity of Christ, is not compatible with the Catholic faith.[33]

11. Similarly, the doctrine of faith regarding the unicity of the salvific economy willed by the One and Triune God must be *firmly believed,* at the source and centre of which is the mystery of the incarnation of the Word, mediator of divine grace on the level of creation and redemption (cf. *Col* 1:15-20), he who recapitulates all things (cf. *Eph* 1:10), he "whom God has made our wisdom, our righteousness, and sanctification and redemption" (*1 Cor* 1:30). In fact, the mystery of Christ has its own intrinsic unity, which extends from the eternal choice in God to the parousia: "he [the Father] chose us in Christ before the foundation of the world to be holy and blameless before him in love" (*Eph* 1:4); "In Christ we are heirs, having been destined according to the purpose of him who accomplishes all things according to his counsel and will" (*Eph* 1:11); "For those

whom he foreknew he also predestined to be conformed to the image of his Son, in order that he might be the first-born among many brothers; those whom he predestined he also called; and those whom he called he also justified; and those whom he justified he also glorified" (*Rom* 8:29-30).

The Church's Magisterium, faithful to divine revelation, reasserts that Jesus Christ is the mediator and the universal redeemer: "The Word of God, through whom all things were made, was made flesh, so that as perfect man he could save all men and sum up all things in himself. The Lord...is he whom the Father raised from the dead, exalted and placed at his right hand, constituting him judge of the living and the dead".[34] This salvific mediation implies also the unicity of the redemptive sacrifice of Christ, eternal high priest (cf. *Heb* 6:20; 9:11; 10:12-14).

12. There are also those who propose the hypothesis of an economy of the Holy Spirit with a more universal breadth than that of the Incarnate Word, crucified and risen. This position also is contrary to the Catholic faith, which, on the contrary, considers the salvific incarnation of the Word as a trinitarian event. In the New Testament, the mystery of Jesus, the Incarnate Word, constitutes the place of the Holy Spirit's presence as well as the principle of the Spirit's effusion on humanity, not only in messianic times (cf. *Acts* 2:32-36; *Jn* 7:39, 20:22; *1 Cor* 15:45), but also prior to his coming in history (cf. *1 Cor* 10:4; *1 Pet* 1:10-12).

The Second Vatican Council has recalled to the consciousness of the Church's faith this fundamental truth. In presenting the Father's salvific plan for all humanity, the Council closely links the mystery of Christ from its very beginnings with that of the Spirit.[35] The entire work of building the Church by Jesus Christ the Head, in the course of the centuries, is seen as an action which he does in communion with his Spirit.[36]

Furthermore, the salvific action of Jesus Christ, with and through his Spirit, extends beyond the visible boundaries of the Church to all humanity. Speaking of the paschal mystery, in which Christ even now associates the believer to himself in a living manner in the Spirit and gives him the hope of resurrection, the Council states: "All this holds true not only for Christians but also for all men of good will in whose hearts grace is active invisibly. For since Christ died for all, and since all men are in fact called to one and the same destiny, which is divine, we must hold that the Holy Spirit offers to all the possibility of being made partners, in a way known to God, in the paschal mystery".[37]

Hence, the connection is clear between the salvific mystery of the Incarnate Word and that of the Spirit, who actualizes the salvific efficacy of the Son made man in the lives of all people, called by God to a single goal, both those who historically preceded the Word made man, and those who live after his coming in history: the Spirit of the Father, bestowed abundantly by the Son, is the animator of all (cf. *Jn* 3:34).

Thus, the recent Magisterium of the Church has firmly and clearly recalled the truth of a single divine economy: "The Spirit's presence and activity affect not only individuals but also society and history, peoples, cultures and religions... The Risen Christ 'is now at work in human hearts through the strength of his Spirit'... Again, it is the Spirit who sows the 'seeds of the word' present in various customs and cultures, preparing them for full maturity in Christ".[38] While recognizing the historical-salvific function of the Spirit in the whole universe and in the entire history of humanity,[39] the Magisterium states: "This is the same Spirit who was at work in the incarnation and in the life, death, and resurrection of Jesus and who is at work in the Church. He is therefore not an alternative to Christ nor does he fill a sort of void which is sometimes suggested as existing between Christ and the Logos. Whatever the Spirit brings about in human hearts and in the history of peoples, in cultures and religions, serves as a preparation for the Gospel and can only be understood in reference to Christ, the Word who took flesh by the power of the Spirit 'so that as perfectly human he would save all human beings and sum up all things'".[40]

In conclusion, the action of the Spirit is not outside or parallel to the action of Christ. There is only one salvific economy of the One and Triune God, realized in the mystery of the incarnation, death, and resurrection of the Son of God, actualized with the cooperation of the Holy Spirit, and extended in its salvific value to all humanity and to the entire universe: "No one, therefore, can enter into communion with God except through Christ, by the working of the Holy Spirit".[41]

III. UNICITY AND UNIVERSALITY OF THE SALVIFIC MYSTERY OF JESUS CHRIST

13. The thesis which denies the unicity and salvific universality of the mystery of Jesus Christ is also put forward. Such a position has no biblical foundation. In fact, the truth of Jesus Christ, Son of God, Lord and only Savior, who through the event of his incarnation, death and resurrection has brought the history of salvation to fulfillment, and which has in him its fullness and centre, must be *firmly believed* as a constant element of the Church's faith.

The New Testament attests to this fact with clarity: "The Father has sent his Son as the Savior of the world" (*1 Jn* 4:14); "Behold the Lamb of God who takes away the sin of the world" (*Jn* 1:29). In his discourse before the Sanhedrin, Peter, in order to justify the healing of a man who was crippled from birth, which was done in the name of Jesus (cf. *Acts* 3:1-8), proclaims: "There is salvation in no one else, for there is no other name under heaven given among men by which we must be saved" (*Acts* 4:12). St. Paul adds, moreover, that Jesus Christ "is Lord of all", "judge of the living and the dead", and thus "whoever believes in him receives forgiveness of sins through his name" (*Acts* 10: 36,42,43).

Paul, addressing himself to the community of Corinth, writes: "Indeed, even though there may be so-called gods in heaven or on earth — as in fact there are many gods and many lords — yet for us there is one God, the Father, from whom are all things and for whom we exist, and one Lord, Jesus Christ, through whom are all things and through whom we exist" (*1 Cor* 8:5-6). Furthermore, John the Apostle states: "For God so loved the world that he gave his only Son, so that everyone who believes in him may not perish but may have eternal life. God did not send his Son into the world to condemn the world, but in order that the world might be saved through him" (*Jn* 3:16-17). In the New Testament, the universal salvific will of God is closely connected to the sole mediation of Christ: "[God] desires all men to be saved and to come to the knowledge of the truth. For there is one God; there is also one mediator between God and men, the man Jesus Christ, who gave himself as a ransom for all" (*1 Tim* 2:4-6).

It was in the awareness of the one universal gift of salvation offered by the Father through Jesus Christ in the Spirit (cf. *Eph* 1:3-14), that the first Christians encountered the Jewish people, showing them the fulfillment of salvation that went beyond the Law and, in the same awareness, they confronted the pagan world of their time, which aspired to salvation through a plurality of saviors. This inheritance of faith has been recalled recently by the Church's Magisterium: "The Church believes that Christ, who died and was raised for the sake of all (cf. *2 Cor* 5:15) can, through his Spirit, give man the light and the strength to be able to respond to his highest calling, nor is there any other name under heaven given among men by which they can be saved (cf. *Acts* 4:12). The Church likewise believes that the key, the centre, and the purpose of the whole of man's history is to be found in its Lord and Master".[42]

14.   It must therefore be *firmly believed* as a truth of Catholic faith that the universal salvific will of the One and Triune God is offered and accomplished once for all in the mystery of the incarnation, death, and resurrection of the Son of God.

Bearing in mind this article of faith, theology today, in its reflection on the existence of other religious experiences and on their meaning in God's salvific plan, is invited to explore if and in what way the historical figures and positive elements of these religions may fall within the divine plan of salvation. In this undertaking, theological research has a vast field of work under the guidance of the Church's Magisterium. The Second Vatican Council, in fact, has stated that: "the unique mediation of the Redeemer does not exclude, but rather gives rise to a manifold cooperation which is but a participation in this one source".[43] The content of this participated mediation should be explored more deeply, but must remain always consistent with the principle of Christ's unique mediation: "Although participated forms of mediation of different kinds and degrees are not excluded, they acquire meaning and value *only* from Christ's own mediation, and they cannot be understood as parallel or complementary to his".[44] Hence, those solutions that propose a salvific action of God beyond the unique mediation of Christ would be contrary to Christian and Catholic faith.

15. Not infrequently it is proposed that theology should avoid the use of terms like "unicity", "universality", and "absoluteness", which give the impression of excessive emphasis on the significance and value of the salvific event of Jesus Christ in relation to other religions. In reality, however, such language is simply being faithful to revela-

tion, since it represents a development of the sources of the faith themselves. From the beginning, the community of believers has recognized in Jesus a salvific value such that he alone, as Son of God made man, crucified and risen, by the mission received from the Father and in the power of the Holy Spirit, bestows revelation (cf. *Mt* 11:27) and divine life (cf. *Jn* 1:12; 5:25-26; 17:2) to all humanity and to every person.

In this sense, one can and must say that Jesus Christ has a significance and a value for the human race and its history, which are unique and singular, proper to him alone, exclusive, universal, and absolute. Jesus is, in fact, the Word of God made man for the salvation of all. In expressing this consciousness of faith, the Second Vatican Council teaches: "The Word of God, through whom all things were made, was made flesh, so that as perfect man he could save all men and sum up all things in himself. The Lord is the goal of human history, the focal point of the desires of history and civilization, the centre of mankind, the joy of all hearts, and the fulfillment of all aspirations. It is he whom the Father raised from the dead, exalted and placed at his right hand, constituting him judge of the living and the dead".[45] "It is precisely this uniqueness of Christ which gives him an absolute and universal significance whereby, while belonging to history, he remains history's centre and goal: 'I am the Alpha and the Omega, the first and the last, the beginning and the end' (*Rev* 22:13)".[46]

IV. UNICITY AND UNITY OF THE CHURCH

16. The Lord Jesus, the only Savior, did not only establish a simple community of disciples, but constituted the Church as a *salvific mystery:* he himself is in the Church and the Church is in him (cf. *Jn* 15:1ff.; *Gal* 3:28; *Eph* 4:15-16; *Acts* 9:5). Therefore, the fullness of Christ's salvific mystery belongs also to the Church, inseparably united to her Lord. Indeed, Jesus Christ continues his presence and his work of salvation in the Church and by means of the Church (cf. *Col* 1:24-27),[47] which is his body (cf. *1 Cor* 12:12-13, 27; *Col* 1:18).[48] And thus, just as the head and members of a living body, though not identical, are inseparable, so too Christ and the Church can neither be confused nor separated, and constitute a single "whole Christ".[49] This same inseparability is also expressed in the New Testament by the analogy of the Church as the *Bride* of Christ (cf. *2 Cor* 11:2; *Eph* 5:25-29; *Rev* 21:2,9).[50]

Therefore, in connection with the unicity and universality of the salvific mediation of Jesus Christ, the unicity of the Church founded by him must be *firmly believed* as a truth of Catholic faith. Just as there is one Christ, so there exists a single body of Christ, a single Bride of Christ: "a single Catholic and apostolic Church".[51] Furthermore, the promises of the Lord that he would not abandon his Church (cf. *Mt* 16:18; 28:20) and that he would guide her by his Spirit (cf. *Jn* 16:13) mean, according to Catholic faith, that the unicity and the unity of the Church — like everything that belongs to the Church's integrity — will never be lacking.[52]

The Catholic faithful *are required to profess* that there is an historical continuity — rooted in the apostolic succession[53] — between the Church founded by Christ and the Catholic Church: "This is the single Church of Christ... which our Savior, after his resurrection, entrusted to Peter's pastoral care (cf. *Jn* 21:17), commissioning him and the other Apostles to extend and rule her (cf. *Mt* 28:18ff.), erected for all ages as 'the pillar and mainstay of the truth' (*1 Tim* 3:15). This Church, constituted and organized as a society in the present world, subsists in [*subsistit in*] the Catholic Church, governed by the Successor of Peter and by the Bishops in communion with him".[54] With the expression *subsistit in,* the Second Vatican Council sought to harmonize two doctrinal statements: on the one hand, that the Church of Christ, despite the divisions which exist among Christians, continues to exist fully only in the Catholic Church, and on the other hand, that "outside of her structure, many elements can be found of sanctification and truth",[55] that is, in those Churches and ecclesial communities which are not yet in full communion with the Catholic Church.[56] But with respect to these, it needs to be stated that "they derive their efficacy from the very fullness of grace and truth entrusted to the Catholic Church".[57]

17.   Therefore, there exists a single Church of Christ, which subsists in the Catholic Church, governed by the Successor of Peter and by the Bishops in communion with him.[58] The Churches which, while not existing in perfect communion with the Catholic Church, remain united to her by means of the closest bonds, that is, by apostolic succession and a valid Eucharist, are true particular Churches.[59] Therefore, the Church of Christ is present and operative also in these Churches, even though they lack full communion with the Catholic Church, since they do not accept the Catholic doctrine of the Primacy, which, according to the will of God, the Bishop of Rome objectively has and exercises over the entire Church.[60]

On the other hand, the ecclesial communities which have not preserved the valid Episcopate and the genuine and integral substance of the Eucharistic mystery,[61] are not Churches in the proper sense; however, those who are baptized in these communities are, by Baptism, incorporated in Christ and thus are in a certain communion, albeit imperfect, with the Church.[62] Baptism in fact tends per se toward the full development of life in Christ, through the integral profession of faith, the Eucharist, and full communion in the Church.[63]

"The Christian faithful are therefore not permitted to imagine that the Church of Christ is nothing more than a collection — divided, yet in some way one — of Churches and ecclesial communities; nor are they free to hold that today the Church of Christ nowhere really exists, and must be considered only as a goal which all Churches and ecclesial communities must strive to reach".[64] In fact, "the elements of this already-given Church exist, joined together in their fullness in the Catholic Church and, without this fullness, in the other communities".[65] "Therefore, these separated Churches and communities as such, though we believe they suffer from defects, have by no means been deprived of significance and importance in the mystery of salvation. For the spirit of Christ has not refrained from using them as means of salvation which derive their efficacy from the very fullness of grace and truth entrusted to the Catholic Church".[66]

The lack of unity among Christians is certainly a *wound* for the Church; not in the sense that she is deprived of her unity, but "in that it hinders the complete fulfillment of her universality in history".[67]

V. THE CHURCH: KINGDOM OF GOD AND KINGDOM OF CHRIST

18. The mission of the Church is "to proclaim and establish among all peoples the kingdom of Christ and of God, and she is on earth, the seed and the beginning of that kingdom".[68] On the one hand, the Church is "a sacrament — that is, sign and instrument of intimate union with God and of unity of the entire human race".[69] She is therefore the sign and instrument of the kingdom; she is called to announce and to establish the kingdom. On the other hand, the Church is the "people gathered by the unity of the Father, the Son and the Holy Spirit";[70] she is therefore "the kingdom of Christ already present in mystery"[71] and constitutes its *seed* and *beginning*. The kingdom of God, in fact, has an eschatological dimension: it is a reality present in time, but its full realization will arrive only with the completion or fulfillment of history.[72]

The meaning of the expressions *kingdom of heaven, kingdom of God*, and *kingdom of Christ* in Sacred Scripture and the Fathers of the Church, as well as in the documents of the Magisterium, is not always exactly the same, nor is their relationship to the Church, which is a mystery that cannot be totally contained by a human concept. Therefore, there can be various theological explanations of these terms. However, none of these possible explanations can deny or empty in any way the intimate connection between Christ, the kingdom, and the Church. In fact, the kingdom of God which we know from revelation, "cannot be detached either from Christ or from the Church... If the kingdom is separated from Jesus, it is no longer the kingdom of God which he revealed. The result is a distortion of the meaning of the kingdom, which runs the risk of being transformed into a purely human or ideological goal and a distortion of the identity of Christ, who no longer appears as the Lord to whom everything must one day be subjected (cf. *1 Cor* 15:27). Likewise, one may not separate the kingdom from the Church. It is true that the Church is not an end unto herself, since she is ordered toward the kingdom of God, of which she is the seed, sign and instrument. Yet, while remaining distinct from Christ and the kingdom, the Church is indissolubly united to both".[73]

19. To state the inseparable relationship between Christ and the kingdom is not to overlook the fact that the kingdom of God — even if considered in its historical phase — is not identified with the Church in her visible and social reality. In fact, "the action of Christ and the Spirit outside the Church's visible boundaries" must not be excluded.[74] Therefore, one must also bear in mind that "the kingdom is the concern of everyone: individuals, society and the world. Working for the kingdom means acknowledging and promoting God's activity, which is present in human history and transforms it. Building the kingdom means working for liberation from evil in all its forms. In a word, the kingdom

of God is the manifestation and the realization of God's plan of salvation in all its fullness".[75]

In considering the relationship between the kingdom of God, the kingdom of Christ, and the Church, it is necessary to avoid one-sided accentuations, as is the case with those "conceptions which deliberately emphasize the kingdom and which describe themselves as 'kingdom centered.' They stress the image of a Church which is not concerned about herself, but which is totally concerned with bearing witness to and serving the kingdom. It is a 'Church for others,' just as Christ is the 'man for others'... Together with positive aspects, these conceptions often reveal negative aspects as well. First, they are silent about Christ: the kingdom of which they speak is 'theocentrically' based, since, according to them, Christ cannot be understood by those who lack Christian faith, whereas different peoples, cultures, and religions are capable of finding common ground in the one divine reality, by whatever name it is called. For the same reason, they put great stress on the mystery of creation, which is reflected in the diversity of cultures and beliefs, but they keep silent about the mystery of redemption. Furthermore, the kingdom, as they understand it, ends up either leaving very little room for the Church or undervaluing the Church in reaction to a presumed 'ecclesiocentrism' of the past and because they consider the Church herself only a sign, for that matter a sign not without ambiguity".[76] These theses are contrary to Catholic faith because they deny the unicity of the relationship which Christ and the Church have with the kingdom of God.

VI. THE CHURCH AND THE OTHER RELIGIONS IN RELATION TO SALVATION

20. From what has been stated above, some points follow that are necessary for theological reflection as it explores the relationship of the Church and the other religions to salvation.

Above all else, it must be *firmly believed* that "the Church, a pilgrim now on earth, is necessary for salvation: the one Christ is the mediator and the way of salvation; he is present to us in his body which is the Church. He himself explicitly asserted the necessity of faith and baptism (cf. *Mk* 16:16; *Jn* 3:5), and thereby affirmed at the same time the necessity of the Church which men enter through baptism as through a door".[77] This doctrine must not be set against the universal salvific will of God (cf. *1 Tim* 2:4); "it is necessary to keep these two truths together, namely, the real possibility of salvation in Christ for all mankind and the necessity of the Church for this salvation".[78]

The Church is the "universal sacrament of salvation",[79] since, united always in a mysterious way to the Savior Jesus Christ, her Head, and subordinated to him, she has, in God's plan, an indispensable relationship with the salvation of every human being.[80] For those who are not formally and visibly members of the Church, "salvation in Christ is accessible by virtue of a grace which, while having a mysterious relationship to the Church, does not make them formally part of the Church, but enlightens them in a way which is accommodated to their spiritual and material situation. This grace comes from Christ; it is the result of his sacrifice and is communicated by the Holy Spirit";[81] it has a relationship with the Church, which "according to the plan of the Father, has her origin in the mission of the Son and the Holy Spirit".[82]

21. With respect to the *way* in which the salvific grace of God — which is always given by means of Christ in the Spirit and has a mysterious relationship to the Church — comes to individual non-Christians, the Second Vatican Council limited itself to the statement that God bestows it "in ways known to himself".[83] Theologians are seeking to understand this question more fully. Their work is to be encouraged, since it is certainly useful for understanding better God's salvific plan and the ways in which it is accomplished. However, from what has been stated above about the mediation of Jesus Christ and the "unique and special relationship"[84] which the Church has with the king-

dom of God among men — which in substance is the universal kingdom of Christ the Savior — it is clear that it would be contrary to the faith to consider the Church as *one way* of salvation alongside those constituted by the other religions, seen as complementary to the Church or substantially equivalent to her, even if these are said to be converging with the Church toward the eschatological kingdom of God.

Certainly, the various religious traditions contain and offer religious elements which come from God,[85] and which are part of what "the Spirit brings about in human hearts and in the history of peoples, in cultures, and religions".[86] Indeed, some prayers and rituals of the other religions may assume a role of preparation for the Gospel, in that they are occasions or pedagogical helps in which the human heart is prompted to be open to the action of God. [87] One cannot attribute to these, however, a divine origin or an *ex opere operato* salvific efficacy, which is proper to the Christian sacraments.[88] Furthermore, it cannot be overlooked that other rituals, insofar as they depend on superstitions or other errors (cf. *1 Cor* 10:20-21), constitute an obstacle to salvation.[89]

22. With the coming of the Savior Jesus Christ, God has willed that the Church founded by him be the instrument for the salvation of *all* humanity (cf. *Acts* 17:30-31).[90] This truth of faith does not lessen the sincere respect

which the Church has for the religions of the world, but at the same time, it rules out, in a radical way, that mentality of indifferentism "characterized by a religious relativism which leads to the belief that 'one religion is as good as another'".[91] If it is true that the followers of other religions can receive divine grace, it is also certain that *objectively speaking* they are in a gravely deficient situation in comparison with those who, in the Church, have the fullness of the means of salvation.[92] However, "all the children of the Church should nevertheless remember that their exalted condition results, not from their own merits, but from the grace of Christ. If they fail to respond in thought, word, and deed to that grace, not only shall they not be saved, but they shall be more severely judged".[93] One understands then that, following the Lord's command (cf. *Mt* 28:19-20) and as a requirement of her love for all people, the Church "proclaims and is in duty bound to proclaim without fail, Christ who is the way, the truth, and the life (*Jn* 14:6). In him, in whom God reconciled all things to himself (cf. *2 Cor* 5:18-19), men find the fullness of their religious life".[94]

In inter-religious dialogue as well, the mission *ad gentes* "today as always retains its full force and necessity".[95] "Indeed, God 'desires all men to be saved and come to the knowledge of the truth' (*1 Tim* 2:4); that is, God wills the salvation of everyone through the knowledge of the truth. Salvation is found in the truth. Those who obey the promptings of the Spirit of truth are already on the way of salvation. But the Church, to whom this truth has been entrusted, must go out to meet their desire, so as to bring them the truth. Because she believes in God's universal plan of salvation, the Church must be missionary".[96] Inter-religious dialogue, therefore, as part of her evangelizing mission, is just one of the actions of the Church in her mission *ad gentes.*[97] *Equality,* which is a presupposition of inter-religious dialogue, refers to the equal personal dignity of the parties in dialogue, not to doctrinal content, nor even less to the position of Jesus Christ — who is God himself made man — in relation to the founders of the other religions. Indeed, the Church, guided by charity and respect for freedom,[98] must be primarily committed to proclaiming to all people the truth definitively revealed by the Lord, and to announcing the necessity of conversion to Jesus Christ and of adherence to the Church through Baptism and the other sacraments, in order to participate fully in communion with God, the Father, Son and Holy Spirit. Thus, the certainty of the universal salvific will of God does not diminish, but rather increases the duty and urgency of the proclamation of salvation and of conversion to the Lord Jesus Christ.

CONCLUSION

23. The intention of the present *Declaration,* in reiterating and clarifying certain truths of the faith, has been to follow the example of the Apostle Paul, who wrote to the faithful of Corinth: "I handed on to you as of first importance what I myself received" (*1 Cor* 15:3). Faced with certain problematic and even erroneous propositions, theological reflection is called to reconfirm the Church's faith and to give reasons for her hope in a way that is convincing and effective.

In treating the question of the true religion, the Fathers of the Second Vatican Council taught: "We believe that this one true religion continues to exist in the Catholic and Apostolic Church, to which the Lord Jesus entrusted the task of spreading it among all people. Thus, he said to the Apostles: 'Go therefore and make disciples of all nations baptizing them in the name of the Father and of the Son and of the Holy Spirit, teaching them to observe all that I have commanded you' (*Mt* 28: 19-20). Especially in those things that concern God and his Church, all persons are required to seek the truth, and when they come to know it, to embrace it and hold fast to it".[99]

The revelation of Christ will continue to be "the true lodestar" [100] in history for all humanity: "The truth, which is Christ, imposes itself as an all-embracing authority". [101]

The Christian mystery, in fact, overcomes all barriers of time and space, and accomplishes the unity of the human family: "From their different locations and traditions all are called in Christ to share in the unity of the family of God's children... Jesus destroys the walls of division and creates unity in a new and unsurpassed way through our sharing in his mystery. This unity is so deep that the Church can say with Saint Paul: 'You are no longer strangers and sojourners, but you are saints and members of the household of God' (*Eph* 2:19)". [102]

The Sovereign Pontiff John Paul II, at the Audience of June 16, 2000, granted to the undersigned Cardinal Prefect of the Congregation for the Doctrine of the Faith, with sure knowledge and by his apostolic authority, ratified and confirmed this Declaration, adopted in Plenary Session and ordered its publication.

Rome, from the Offices of the Congregation for the Doctrine of the Faith, August 6, 2000, the Feast of the Transfiguration of the Lord.

Joseph Card. Ratzinger
Prefect

Tarcisio Bertone, S.D.B.
Archbishop Emeritus of Vercelli
Secretary

NOTES

(1) First Council of Constantinople, *Symbolum Constantinopolitanum*: *DS* 150.

(2) Cf. John Paul II, Encyclical Letter *Redemptoris missio*, 1: *AAS* 83 (1991), 249-340.

(3) Cf. Second Vatican Council, Decree *Ad gentes* and Declaration *Nostra aetate*; cf. also Paul VI Apostolic Exhortation *Evangelii nuntiandi*: *AAS* 68 (1976), 5-76; John Paul II, Encyclical Letter *Redemptoris missio*.

(4) Second Vatican Council, Declaration *Nostra aetate*, 2.

(5) Pontifical Council for Inter-religious Dialogue and the Congregation for the Evangelization of Peoples, Instruction *Dialogue and Proclamation*, 29: *AAS* 84 (1992), 424; cf. Second Vatican Council, Pastoral Constitution *Gaudium et spes*, 22.

(6) Cf. John Paul II, Encyclical Letter *Redemptoris missio*, 55: *AAS* 83 (1991), 302-304.

(7) Cf. Pontifical Council for Inter-religious Dialogue and the Congregation for the Evangelization of Peoples, Instruction *Dialogue and Proclamation*, 9: *AAS* 84 (1992), 417ff.

(8) John Paul II, Encyclical Letter *Fides et ratio*, 5: *AAS* 91 (1999), 5-88.

(9) Second Vatican Council, Dogmatic Constitution *Dei verbum*, 2.

(10) *Ibid.*, 4.

(11) John Paul II, Encyclical Letter *Redemptoris missio*, 5.

(12) John Paul II, Encyclical Letter *Fides et ratio*, 14.

(13) Council of Chalcedon, *Symbolum Chalcedonense*: *DS* 301; cf. St. Athanasius, *De Incarnatione*, 54, 3: *SC* 199, 458.

(14) Second Vatican Council, Dogmatic Constitution *Dei verbum*, 4.

(15) *Ibid.*, 5.

(16) *Ibid.*

(17) Cf. *Catechism of the Catholic Church*, 144.

(18) *Ibid.*, 150.

(19) *Ibid.*, 153.

(20) *Ibid.*, 178.

(21) John Paul II, Encyclical Letter *Fides et ratio*, 13.

(22) Cf. *ibid.*, 31-32.

(23) Second Vatican Council, Declaration *Nostra aetate*, 2; cf. Second Vatican Council, Decree *Ad gentes*, 9, where it speaks of the elements of good present "in the particular customs and cultures of peoples"; Dogmatic Constitution *Lumen gentium*, 16, where it mentions the elements of good and of truth present among non-Christians, which can be considered a preparation for the reception of the Gospel.

(24) Cf. Council of Trent, *Decretum de libris sacris et de traditionibus recipiendis*: DS 1501; First Vatican Council, Dogmatic Constitution *Dei Filius*, cap. 2: DS 3006.

(25) Second Vatican Council, Dogmatic Constitution *Dei verbum*, 11.

(26) *Ibid.*

(27) John Paul II, Encyclical Letter *Redemptoris missio*, 55; cf. 56 and Paul VI, Apostolic Exhortation *Evangelii nuntiandi*, 53.

(28) First Council of Nicaea, *Symbolum Nicaenum*: DS 125.

(29) Council of Chalcedon, *Symbolum Chalcedonense*: DS 301.

(30) Second Vatican Council, Pastoral Constitution *Gaudium et spes*, 22.

(31) John Paul II, Encyclical Letter *Redemptoris missio*, 6.

(32) Cf. St. Leo the Great, *Tomus ad Flavianum*: DS 294.

(33) Cf. St. Leo the Great, Letter to the Emperor Leo I *Promisisse me memini*: DS 318: "*...in tantam unitatem ab ipso conceptu Virginis deitate et humanitate conserta, ut nec sine homine divina, nec sine Deo agerentur humana*". Cf. also *ibid.* DS 317.

(34) Second Vatican Council, Pastoral Constitution *Gaudium et spes*, 45; cf. also Council of Trent, *Decretum de peccato originali*, 3: *DS* 1513.

(35) Cf. Second Vatican Council, Dogmatic Constitution *Lumen gentium*, 3-4.

(36) Cf. *ibid.*, 7; cf. St. Irenaeus, who wrote that it is in the Church "that communion with Christ has been deposited, that is to say: the Holy Spirit" (*Adversus haereses* III, 24, 1: *SC* 211, 472).

(37) Second Vatican Council, Pastoral Constitution *Gaudium et spes*, 22.

(38) John Paul II, Encyclical Letter *Redemptoris missio*, 28. For the "seeds of the Word" cf. also St. Justin Martyr, *Second Apology* 8, 1-2; 10, 1-3; 13, 3-6: ed. E.J. Goodspeed, 84; 85; 88-89.

(39) Cf. John Paul II, Encyclical Letter, *Redemptoris missio*, 28-29.

(40) *Ibid.*, 29.

(41) *Ibid.*, 5.

(42) Second Vatican Council, Pastoral Constitution *Gaudium et spes*, 10. Cf. St. Augustine, who wrote that Christ is the way, which "has never been lacking to mankind... and apart from this way no one has been set free, no one is being set free, no one will be set free" *De civitate Dei* 10, 32, 2: *CCSL* 47, 312.

(43) Second Vatican Council, Dogmatic Constitution *Lumen gentium*, 62.

(44) John Paul II, Encyclical Letter *Redemptoris missio*, 5.

(45) Second Vatican Council, Pastoral Constitution *Gaudium et spes*, 45. The necessary and absolute singularity of Christ in human history is well expressed by St. Irenaeus in contemplating the preeminence of Jesus as firstborn Son: "In the heavens, as firstborn of the Father's counsel, the perfect Word governs and legislates all things; on the earth, as firstborn of the Virgin, a man just and holy, reverencing God and pleasing to God, good and perfect in every way, he saves from hell all those who follow him since he is the firstborn from the dead and Author of the life of God" (*Demonstratio apostolica*, 39: *SC* 406, 138).

(46) John Paul II, Encyclical Letter *Redemptoris missio*, 6.

(47) Cf. Second Vatican Council, Dogmatic Constitution *Lumen gentium*, 14.

(48) Cf. *ibid.*, 7.

(49) Cf. St. Augustine, *Enarratio in Psalmos,* Ps. 90, *Sermo* 2,1: *CCSL* 39, 1266; St. Gregory the Great, *Moralia in Iob,* Praefatio, 6, 14: *PL* 75, 525; St. Thomas Aquinas, *Summa Theologiae,* III, q. 48, a. 2 ad 1.

(50) Cf. Second Vatican Council, Dogmatic Constitution *Lumen gentium,* 6.

(51) *Symbolum maius Ecclesiae Armeniacae*: *DS* 48. Cf. Boniface VIII, *Unam sanctam*: *DS* 870-872; Second Vatican Council, Dogmatic Constitution *Lumen gentium,* 8.

(52) Cf. Second Vatican Council, Decree *Unitatis redintegratio,* 4; John Paul II, Encyclical Letter *Ut unum sint,* 11: *AAS* 87 (1995), 927.

(53) Cf. Second Vatican Council, Dogmatic Constitution *Lumen gentium,* 20; cf. also St. Irenaeus, *Adversus haereses,* III, 3, 1-3: *SC* 211, 20-44; St. Cyprian, *Epist.* 33, 1: *CCSL* 3B, 164-165; St. Augustine, *Contra adver. legis et prophet.,* 1, 20, 39: *CCSL* 49, 70.

(54) Second Vatican Council, Dogmatic Constitution *Lumen gentium,* 8.

(55) *Ibid.*; cf. John Paul II, Encyclical Letter *Ut unum sint,* 13. Cf. also Second Vatican Council, Dogmatic Constitution *Lumen gentium,* 15 and the Decree *Unitatis redintegratio,* 3.

(56) The interpretation of those who would derive from the formula *subsistit in* the thesis that the one Church of Christ could subsist also in non-Catholic Churches and ecclesial communities is therefore contrary to the authentic meaning of *Lumen gentium.* "The Council instead chose the word *subsistit* precisely to clarify that there exists only one 'subsistence' of the true Church, while outside her visible structure there only exist *elementa Ecclesiae,* which — being elements of that same Church — tend and lead toward the Catholic Church" (Congregation for the Doctrine of the Faith, *Notification on the Book "Church: Charism and Power" by Father Leonardo Boff*: *AAS* 77 [1985], 756-762).

(57) Second Vatican Council, Decree *Unitatis redintegratio,* 3.

(58) Cf. Congregation for the Doctrine of the Faith, Declaration *Mysterium Ecclesiae,* 1: *AAS* 65 (1973), 396-398.

(59) Cf. Second Vatican Council, Decree *Unitatis redintegratio,* 14 and 15; Congregation for the Doctrine of the Faith, Letter *Communionis notio,* 17: *AAS* 85 (1993), 848.

(60) Cf. First Vatican Council, Constitution *Pastor aeternus*: *DS* 3053-3064; Second Vatican Council, Dogmatic Constitution *Lumen gentium*, 22.

(61) Cf. Second Vatican Council, Decree *Unitatis redintegratio*, 22.

(62) Cf. *ibid.*, 3.

(63) Cf. *ibid.*, 22.

(64) Congregation for the Doctrine of the Faith, Declaration *Mysterium Ecclesiae*, 1.

(65) John Paul II, Encyclical Letter *Ut unum sint*, 14.

(66) Second Vatican Council, Decree *Unitatis redintegratio*, 3.

(67) Congregation for the Doctrine of the Faith, Letter *Communionis notio*, 17; cf. Second Vatican Council, Decree *Unitatis redintegratio*, 4.

(68) Second Vatican Council, Dogmatic Constitution *Lumen gentium*, 5.

(69) *Ibid.*, 1.

(70) *Ibid.*, 4. Cf. St. Cyprian, *De Dominica oratione* 23: *CCSL* 3A, 105.

(71) Second Vatican Council, Dogmatic Constitution *Lumen gentium*, 3.

(72) Cf. *ibid.*, 9; cf. also the prayer addressed to God found in the *Didache* 9,4: *SC* 248, 176: "May the Church be gathered from the ends of the earth into your kingdom" and *ibid.* 10, 5: *SC* 248, 180: "Remember, Lord, your Church... and, made holy, gather her together from the four winds into your kingdom which you have prepared for her".

(73) John Paul II, Encyclical Letter *Redemptoris missio*, 18; cf. Apostolic Exhortation *Ecclesia in Asia*, 17: *L'Osservatore Romano* (November 7, 1999). The kingdom is so inseparable from Christ that, in a certain sense, it is identified with him (cf. Origen, *In Mt. Hom.*, 14, 7: *PG* 13, 1197; Tertullian, *Adversus Marcionem*, IV, 33,8: *CCSL* 1, 634.

(74) John Paul II, Encyclical Letter *Redemptoris missio*, 18.

(75) *Ibid.*, 15.

(76) *Ibid.*, 17.

(77) Second Vatican Council, Dogmatic Constitution *Lumen gentium*, 14; cf. Decree *Ad gentes*, 7; Decree *Unitatis redintegratio*, 3.

(78) John Paul II, Encyclical Letter *Redemptoris missio*, 9; cf. *Catechism of the Catholic Church*, 846-847.

(79) Second Vatican Council, Dogmatic Constitution *Lumen gentium*, 48.

(80) Cf. St. Cyprian, *De catholicae ecclesiae unitate*, 6: *CCSL* 3, 253-254; St. Irenaeus, *Adversus haereses*, III, 24, 1: *SC* 211, 472-474.

(81) John Paul II, Encyclical Letter *Redemptoris missio*, 10.

(82) Second Vatican Council, Decree *Ad gentes*, 2. The famous formula *extra Ecclesiam nullus omnino salvatur* is to be interpreted in this sense (cf. Fourth Lateran Council, Cap. 1. *De fide catholica*: DS 802). Cf. also the *Letter of the Holy Office to the Archbishop of Boston*: DS 3866-3872.

(83) Second Vatican Council, Decree *Ad gentes*, 7.

(84) John Paul II, Encyclical Letter *Redemptoris missio*, 18.

(85) These are the seeds of the divine Word (*semina Verbi*), which the Church recognizes with joy and respect (cf. Second Vatican Council, Decree *Ad gentes*, 11; Declaration *Nostra aetate*, 2).

(86) John Paul II, Encyclical Letter *Redemptoris missio*, 29.

(87) Cf. *ibid.; Catechism of the Catholic Church*, 843.

(88) Cf. Council of Trent, *Decretum de sacramentis*, can. 8, *de sacramentis in genere*: DS 1608.

(89) Cf. John Paul II, Encyclical Letter *Redemptoris missio*, 55.

(90) Cf. Second Vatican Council, Dogmatic Constitution *Lumen gentium*, 17; John Paul II, Encyclical Letter *Redemptoris missio*, 11.

(91) John Paul II, Encyclical Letter *Redemptoris missio*, 36.

(92) Cf. Pius XII, Encyclical Letter *Mystici corporis*: DS 3821.

(93) Second Vatican Council, Dogmatic Constitution *Lumen gentium*, 14.

(94) Second Vatican Council, Declaration *Nostra aetate*, 2.

(95) Second Vatican Council, Decree *Ad gentes*, 7.

(96) *Catechism of the Catholic Church*, 851; cf. also 849-856.

(97) Cf. John Paul II, Encyclical Letter *Redemptoris missio*, 55; Apostolic Exhortation *Ecclesia in Asia*, 31.

(98) Cf. Second Vatican Council, Declaration *Dignitatis humanae*, 1.

(99) *Ibid.*

(100) John Paul II, Encyclical Letter *Fides et ratio*, 15.

(101) *Ibid.*, 92.

(102) *Ibid.*, 70.